A YEAR IN PICTURES: 1975

Concept and archive development: **Ted Cockle**

Design: **Jac Harries**

Full gratitude to Christopher Sleet at Getty Images

ISBN: 978-1-3999-9206-0

M·P

**MUSSEL
PUBLICATIONS**

1975 OVERVIEW

This book features the most fun, fascinating, and memorable images of the year 1975.

In the US, the Watergate scandal was a major political scandal that led to President Nixon's resignation and proved to be a constitutional crisis. The Vietnam War ended with the Fall of Saigon. Communist forces from North Vietnam took Saigon, resulting in the mass evacuation of the remaining US troops and South Vietnamese civilians.

In the UK, unemployment reached an all-time high with 1.25 million individuals in the country being jobless, and Britain entered a double-dip recession. The Sex Discrimination Act and the Equal Pay Act came into force, aiming to end unequal pay between men and women in the workplace.

On the roads, the best-selling cars were the Ford Cortina and the Ford Escort. A loaf of bread cost just 11p, a pint of lager was 20p, and a packet of cigarettes was 20p for 20. The average house price in the UK was just £16,980.

By 1975, people were eating out on a regular basis, and the country was now addicted to new spicy foods, with the nation's love affair with chicken tikka masala well and truly begun.

'Jaws' and 'One Flew Over the Cuckoo's Nest' featuring Jack Nicholson were the best-performing films of the year. Elizabeth Taylor and Richard Burton secretly remarried, just 16 months after divorcing.

Please enjoy the journey through all the images that created the full experience of 1975.

CELEBRITIES BORN IN 1975

Bradley Cooper 05/01

Natalie Imbruglia 04/02

Gary Neville 18/02

Drew Barrymore 22/02

Naga Munchetty 25/02

Will.I.Am 15/03

Eva Longoria 15/03

Melanie Blatt 25/03

Fergie 27/03

Robbie Fowler 09/04

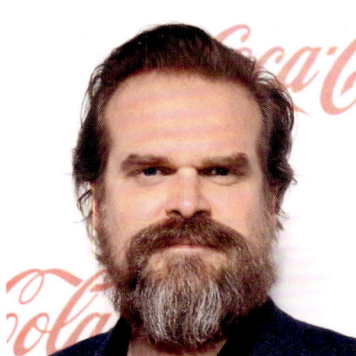

David Harbour 10/04

David Beckham 02/05

Enrique Iglesias 08/05

Jonah Lomu 12/05

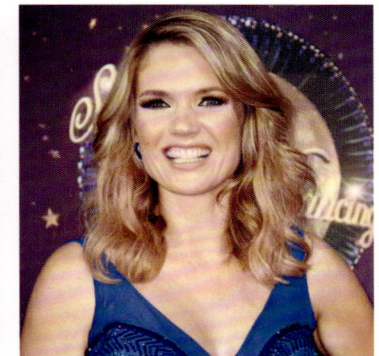

Charlotte Hawkins 16/05

Jack Johnson 18/05

Lauryn Hill 26/05

Jamie Oliver 27/05

Andre 3000 27/05

Mel B 29/05

Angelina Jolie 04/06

KT Tunstall 23/06

Tobey Maguire 27/06

Ralph Schumacher 30/06

50 Cent 06/07

Jack White 09/07

Jill Halfpenny 15/07

Konnie Huq 17/07

Charlize Theron 07/08

Mark Ronson 04/09

Michael Buble 09/09

Declan Connelly 25/09

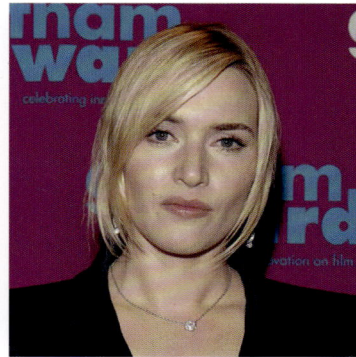

Kate Winslet 05/10

Shaznay Lewis 14/10

Anthony McPartlin 18/10

Sia 18/10

Travis Barker 14/11

Faye Tozer 14/11

Dierks Bentley 20/11

DJ Khaled 26/11

Ronnie O'Sullivan 05/12

Tom Delonge 13/12

Milla Jovovich 17/12

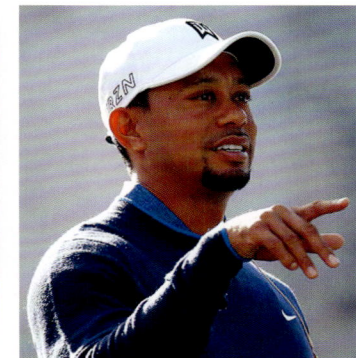

Tiger Woods 30/12

UK LIFE

IRA BOMBINGS

Throughout the year the IRA carried out a major series of bombing on targets across London.

This included a bomb placed under the car of the Conservative MP Hugh Fraser, intended for Caroline Kennedy on Campden Hill Square, a bomb intended for MP John Frost in Connaught Square, the Trattoria Restaurant, Scotts Oyster Restaurant on Mount Street Mayfair and outside Green Park Tube Station.

MP John Frost's car, Connaught Square, London

Trattoria restaurant

Hilton Hotel, Park Lane

MP Sir Hugh Fraser's car, Campden Hill Square, London

Scotts Oyster Restaurant

Green Park Tube Station

NUNEATON RAIL CRASH

In June, there was a major rail crash in Nuneaton, Warwickshire, when the high-speed sleeper service from London Euston to Glasgow derailed.

FREDDY LAKER

English airline entrepreneur Freddie Laker won his legal battle for a licence to run a flight service between London and New York, UK, on 2nd October 1975. His licence had been revoked by the government earlier that year after pressure from established airlines.

LONDON DOCK STRIKES

In February, 9,000 London dock workers went on strike. The strike leader was Bill Nicholson.

EVIL KNIEVEL

The American stunt artist visited Wembley Stadium to attempt to jump thirteen double-decker buses inside the stadium. Knievel ultimately crashed his Harley-Davidson XR-750 on landing, breaking his pelvis and fracturing bones in his hand.

LABOUR PARTY

The Prime Minister, Labour leader Harold Wilson, was voted in following the General Election in October 1974, which resulted in a narrow victory for the Labour Party with a majority of three seats.

His cabinet was made up of Barbara Castle, the Secretary of State for Health and Education, Chancellor of the Exchequer Denis Healey, and Employment Secretary Michael Foot.

In February, Wilson visited US President Gerald Ford in Washington, DC, and met with him again at the NATO summit in Brussels in May.

The following year, Wilson resigned and was replaced by James Callaghan, who had been Foreign & Commonwealth Secretary.

CONSERVATIVE PARTY

In February, Margaret Thatcher defeated Edward Heath for the leadership of the opposition, the UK Conservative Party. Thatcher, aged 49, became Britain's first female leader of any political party.

The Keep Britain In Europe Conference was held at the Waldorf Hotel in May.

Liberal Party **Jeremy Thorpe**
Conservative Party **Edward Heath**
Labour Party **Roy Jenkins**

Labour Party **Shirley Williams**

ROYALTY

QUEEN ELIZABETH

PRINCE CHARLES

The Queen & her mother

Princess Margaret, Lord Snowdon & Elton John

Princess Anne

SPORT

FOOTBALL

In May, West Ham beat Fulham 2-0 in the FA Cup Final at Wembley Stadium. Both goals were scored by Alan Taylor. The West Ham fans invaded the pitch when the match finished.

The team did a victory parade with the FA Cup, arriving at Newham Town Hall with a mounted police escort for their open-top bus.

FULHAM

West Ham legend Bobby Moore appeared for Fulham, where John Lyall served as manager.

DERBY COUNTY

Derby County won the league for the second time in four seasons under the management of Dave Mackay. Colin Todd, Keith Osgood, and Scottish international footballer Archie Gemmill running out onto the pitch before a match for Derby County.

GEORGE BEST

Northern Irish player George Best wore a Chelsea kit during a testimonial match for striker Peter Osgood in November. He was also playing in the US for the Fort Lauderdale Strikers in Florida. Michael Parkinson interviewed George on the 'Today' show.

LIVERPOOL

CHELSEA

NEWCASTLE

ARSENAL

Liverpool finished as runners-up under Bob Paisley after Bill Shankly's retirement in 1974. Emlyn Hughes here walking out.

Chelsea plagued by falling attendances and rising debts were relegated this year. Ray Wilkins here at Stamford Bridge

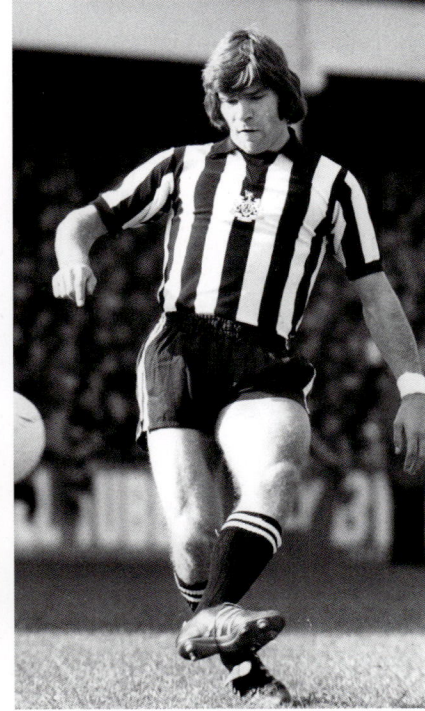

Malcolm MacDonald of Newcastle was the top goalscorer this season with 21 goals.

Arsenal featured the talent of Charlie George here at Highbury.

The Tottenham team included one of the greatest goalkeepers of all time, Northern Ireland international Pat Jennings.

Just two years later, Jennings would transfer to Tottenham's arch-rivals, Arsenal. Glenn Hoddle was another key player at White Hart Lane this season.

BRIAN CLOUGH

Clough, former manager of Derby and Leeds, replaced Allan Brown as manager of struggling Nottingham Forest in January. He signed Scottish duo John McGovern and John O'Hare. He then brought John Robertson and Martin O'Neill back into the fold after they had requested transfers under Brown. Viv Anderson also became a regular under Clough. Here he is in his first game in charge at White Hart Lane against Tottenham Hotspur.

ENGLAND TEAM

Don Revie was now in charge of the England team. The squad featured Kevin Keegan, Peter Shilton, Mick Channon, David Johnson, and David Nish. Alan Hudson and captain Alan Ball pictured playing during England vs West Germany in March.

TENNIS
WIMBLEDON FINAL

In the men's final, Arthur Ashe beat Jimmy Connors.

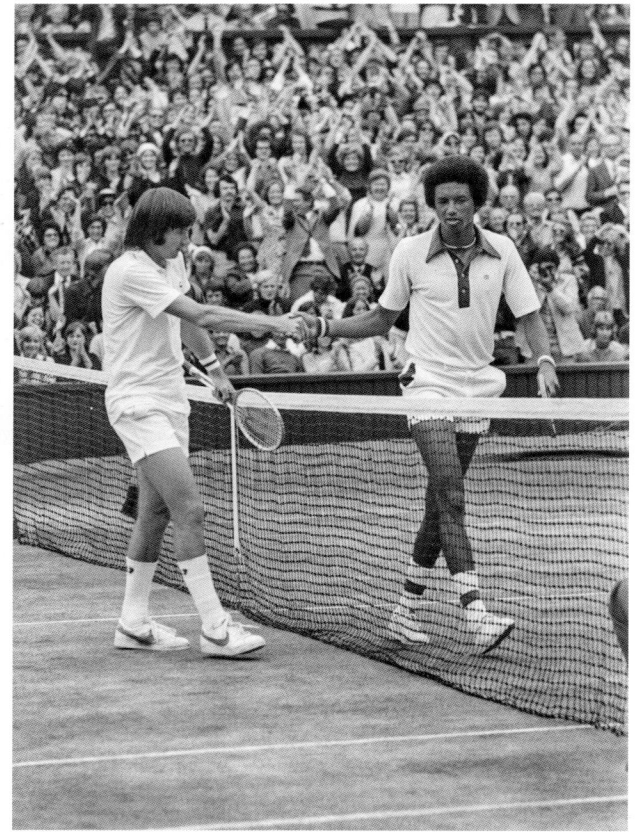

In the women's final, Billie Jean King beat Evonne Goolagong Cawley. It was King's 12th and last career Grand Slam title and her 6th Wimbledon title. King was also heavily involved in the tennis pay parity talks.

Eighteen-year-old Martina Navratilova of Czechoslovakia announced her defection to the United States.

Chris Evert Lloyd won the Women's US Open. In the women's doubles, Ann Kiyomura and Kazuko Sawamatsu beat Françoise Durr and Betty Stove.

GOLF

The US Open this year was won by Lou Graham with John Mahaffey in second place. Tom Watson won the Open in Scotland by one stroke over Jack Nicklaus.

John Mahaffey

Arnold Palmer

Tom Watson

CRICKET

This year, the first-ever Cricket World Cup was held in England. The West Indies won the competition, beating Australia in the final.

Australia toured England and there were 3 draws and one loss, so Australia were victorious and retained the Ashes.

The match at Headingley was abandoned in controversial circumstances when the pitch was destroyed by political protestors. Australia retained the Ashes.

Leicestershire won their first County Championship title.

Leading batsmen in the championship were Rohan Kanhai, Geoffrey Boycott, Clive Lloyd, Doug Walters, Barry Richards, David Steele, Tony Greig, and Mike Brearly.

The leading bowlers were David Steele, Andy Roberts, Mike Hendrick, Bernard Julien, Peter Lever, Peter Lee, Sarfraz Nawaz, John Lever, Bishan Bedi, and Malcolm Nash.

Wicketkeeper Alan Knott and captain Tony Greig celebrate Australian batsman Jeff Thomson being bowled out.

England captain Tony Greig walking with Australian captain Ian Chappell.

Graham Gooch of Kent being bowled out.

BOXING

John Conteh, the World Boxing Council Light Heavyweight champion of Great Britain poses for a portrait at the Allsport studio in London and also alongside his opponent, Lonnie Bennett, at the Dominion Theatre in Tottenham Court Road, London.

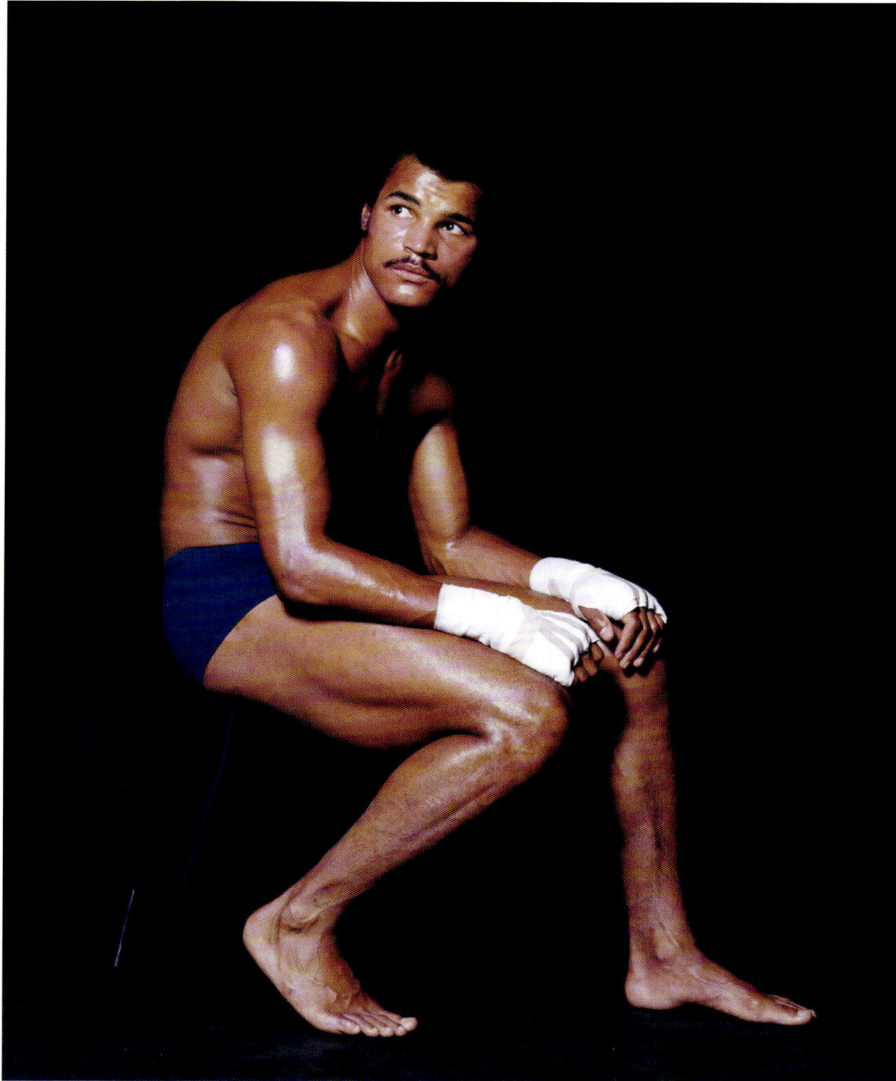

The 'Thrilla In Manila' was the third and final boxing match between undisputed champion Muhammad Ali and former champion Joe Frazier for the heavyweight championship of the world. The bout was concluded after 14 rounds with Ali victorious. It is widely regarded as one of the best and most brutal fights in boxing history, with some sources estimating that over 1 billion people viewed this fight.

Ali fought Joe Frazier in the heavyweight match in Manila, Philippines.

Promotor Don King, alongside Ali and Joe Frazier in New York.

Ali spoke to the international press during a break in his training.

ATHLETICS

Brendan Foster

Competing at Crystal Palace, where Foster won the 5000 metres.

Steve Ovett

GYMNASTICS

Olga Korbut

The Russian gymnast and Olympic gold medal winner.

SNOOKER

Cliff Thorburn

Canadian snooker player at the Benson and Hedges Masters Snooker Championship on 22 January 1975 at Wembley Arena. Ray Reardon beat Eddie Charlton in the end.

BARRY SHEENE

British racing motorcyclist at the Motorcycle Show with his 750cc Heron Suzuki at Earl's Court, and then on the track, taking Becketts corner at speed during the John Player Motorcycle Grand Prix at Silverstone Circuit, Northamptonshire in August. A race which Sheene won.

MOTOR RACING

Driver Graham Hill dies in an air crash in Hertfordshire. At the British Grand Prix at Silverstone, Brazilian driver Emerson Fittipaldi is declared the winner of the John Player Race, after the race was abandoned due to multiple accidents caused by heavy hail and rain. Scheckter, Hunt, and Donohue were all forced to abort.

James Hunt

Hunt & his wife Suzy Miller

Hunt & Jody Scheckter of South Africa

Brazilian Emerson Fittipaldi

CITY LIFE

DH EVANS department store on Oxford Street.

The Camden Theatre, which then became known as Camden Palace and is now known as Koko.

A crowd gathers in Hyde Park.

The Thamsemead estate in the Royal Borough of Greenwich.

Denmark Street in Soho, often also known as Tin Pan Alley.

A business man walking on Park Crescent, elegant stuccoed terraced houses designed by the architecht John Nash on the approach to Regents Park.

The Royal National Theatre under construction on the South Bank.

The original Ivy restaurant located on West Street by Cambridge Circus.

A row of Black London taxi's stuck in traffic on Penton Street, near The Angel.

Commuters on a train platform during rush hour at Earl's Court station.

Victoria Station and the coaches lined up and a man taking a sandwich from a pantry at a cafeteria at the Station.

A tube pulls into Trafalgar Square tube station, which is now known as Charing Cross.

Victoria Station

Somers Town Goods Depot next to St Pancras International Station.

There was a crash at Moorgate Tube station in February.

MUSIC

ALBUMS RELEASED THIS YEAR

Januray	**Bob Dylan**	Blood On The Tracks
February	**Led Zeppelin**	Physical Graffiti
March	**10CC**	The Original Soundtrack
	Jeff Beck	Blow By Blow
	David Bowie	Young Americans
	Earth Wind & Fire	That's The Way Of The World
	Smokey Robinson	A Quiet Storm
	Steely Dan	Katy Lied
April	**Aerosmith**	Toys In The Attic
	Funkadelic	Let's Take It To The Stage
	Parliament	Chocolate City
May	**Elton John**	Captain Fantastic
	Allen Toussaint	Southern Nights
	Wings	Venus And Mars
June	**Bob Dylan**	The Basement Tapes
	Eagles	One Of These Nights
	The Isley Brothers	The Heat Is
	Neil Young	Tonights The Night

July	**Tavares**	In The City
August	**Fleetwood Mac**	Fleetwood Mac
	Ohio Players	Honey
	Bruce Springsteen	Born To Run
	Donna Summer	Love To Love You Baby
	ELO	Face The Music
September	**Pink Floyd**	Wish You Were Here
	Roxy Music	Siren
October	**Paul Simon**	Still Crazy After All These Years
	Tom Waits	Nighthawks At The Diner
	The Who	The Who By Numbers
November	**Brian Eno**	Another Green World
	Harold Melvin + The Blue Notes	Wake Up Everybody
	Joni Mitchell	Hissing Of Summer Lawns
	Queen	A Night At The Opera
	Patti Smith	Horses
December	**Burning Spear**	Marcus Garvey
	Bob Marley	Live

BIGGEST POP SONGS IN 1975

Status Quo	Down Down
Kenny	The Bump
Gloria Gaynor	Never Can Say Goodbye
The Tymes	Ms Grace
Pilot	January
The Glitter Band	Goodbye My love
Mac And Katie Kissoon	Sugar Candy Kisses
The Carpenters	Please Mr Postman
Steve Harley & Cockney Rebel	Make me Smile (Come Up And See Me)
Mud	The Secrets That You Keep
Tellly Salavas	If
Fox	Only You Can
Bay City Rollers	Bye Bye Baby
Guys N Dolls	There's A Whole Lot Of Loving
The Moments & Whatnauts	Girls
Sweet	Fox On The Run
Peter Shelley	Love Me Love My Dog
Bobby Goldsboro	Honey
Mud	O Boy
Minnie Riperton	Lovin' You
Tammy Wynette	Stand By Your Man
Windsor Davies + Don Estelle	Whispering Grass
The Stylistics	Sing Baby Sing
Showaddywaddy	Three Steps To Heaven
10 CC	I'm Not IN Love
Van McCoy	The Hustle
Johnny Nash	Tears On My Pillow
Ray Stevens	Misty
Bay City Rollers	Give A Little Love

Smoke	If You Think You Know How To Love Me
Stylistics	Can't Give You Anything
Roger Whitaker	The Last Farewell
Rod Stewart	Sailing
Leo Sayer	Moonlighting
David Essex	Hold Me Close
The Drifters	There Goes My First Love
Art Garfunkel	I Only Have Eyes For You
David Bowie	Space Oddity
Roxy Music	Love Is The Drug
Glen Campbell	Rhinestone Cowboy
Billy Connolly	DIVORCE
Hot Chocolate	You Sexy Thing
Rod Stewart	This Old Heart Of Mine
Queen	Bohemian Rhapsody
Laurel And Hardy	The Trail Of The Lonesome Pine
Greg Lake	I Believe In Father Christmas

The best selling single of the year was 'Bye Bye Baby' by the Bay City Rollers and the Christmas number one was 'Bohemian Rhapsody' by Queen.

ROD STEWART

Rod spent a lot of time this year with Britt Ekland. He toured the US twice with the Faces, including shows at Madison Square Garden. In August, Rod released his album 'Atlantic Crossing'. The album reached the top ten in the US and number one in the UK. It produced two number one hit singles, 'Sailing' and 'I Don't Want To Talk About It'. In December, he announced that the Faces were splitting up.

With David Bowie

With Pele

THE WHO

PAUL McCARTNEY + WINGS

This was a year when Pete Townshend was dealing with personal issues, which led to a more confessional singer-songwriter album, 'The Who By Numbers', with help from his fellow band members.

This year, Wings released their 'Venus and Mars' album. Now operating as a genuine band, they created rock anthems like 'Rock Show'.

DAVID BOWIE

Following the 'Diamond Dogs' era, Bowie moved heavily towards R&B, and his album this year was 'Young Americans'. This was a full-blown step into the world of blue-eyed soul, fully immersed in the sonics of Philly soul and disco, helped by the likes of Luther Vandross on backing vocals. Key songs include 'Fame' and the title track.

Bowie with Art Garfunkel, Paul Simon, Yoko Ono, John Lennon + Nina Simone.

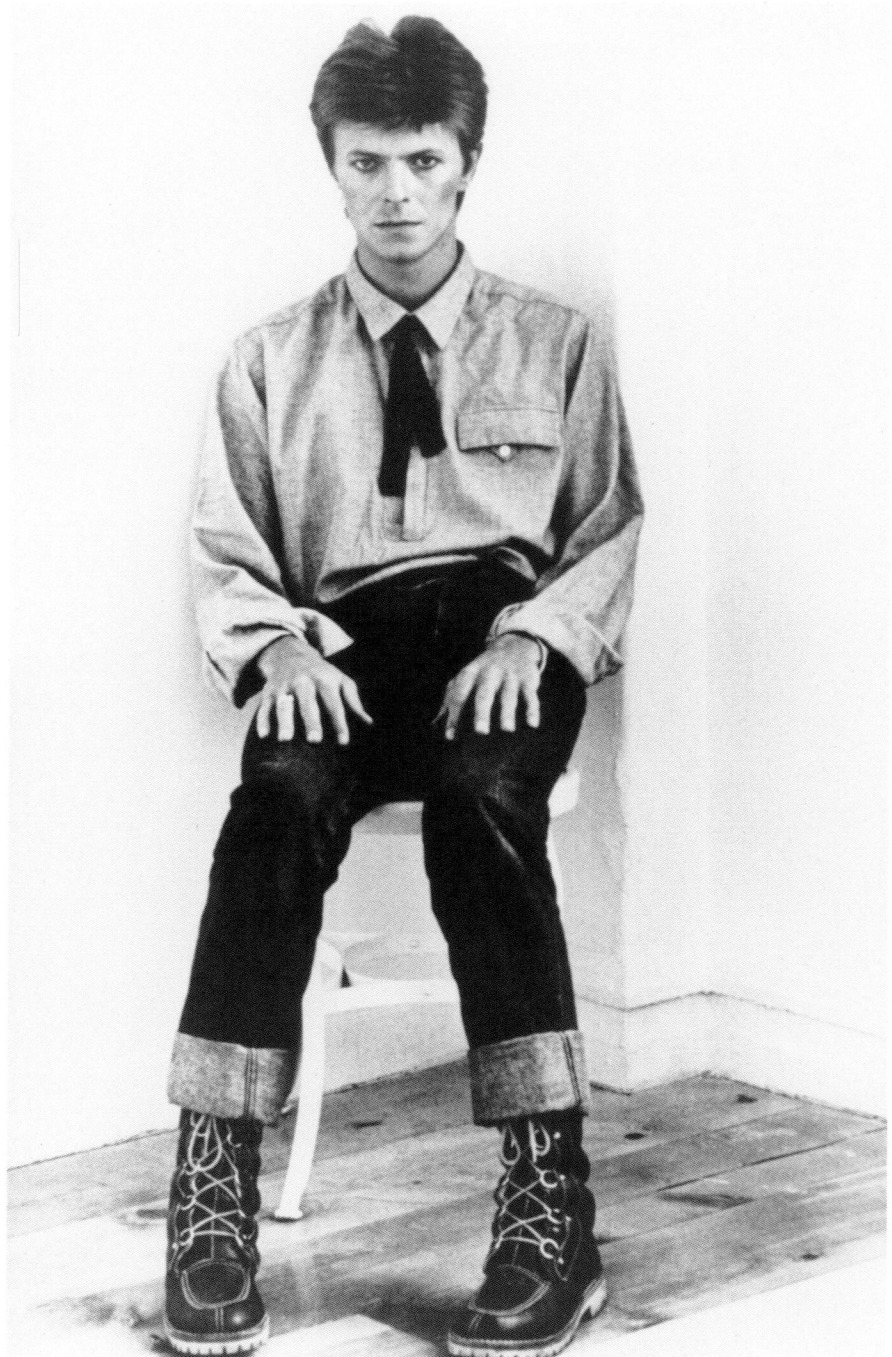

With his wife Angie

TOM JONES

Tom Jones released the album 'Memories Don't Leave Like People Do'.

DAVID ESSEX

The 'All The Fun Of The Fair' was released this year, an album produced by Jeff Wayne and featuring the hit single 'Hold Me Close'.

MICK JAGGER

KEITH RICHARDS

RONNIE WOOD

QUEEN

This year the band released their 'Night At The Opera' album. This was an overblown rock masterpiece featuring the landmark track 'Bohemian Rhapsody'. This six minute song was written by Freddie Mercury. The song topped the singles chart in the UK for nine weeks and has ultimately proved to be one of the best selling songs of all time.

ELTON JOHN

This year, Elton John released his album 'Captain Fantastic'. It charted at number one driven by the big tune 'Someone Saved My Life Tonight'. It also featured Elton's version of the Beatles song 'Lucy In The Sky With Diamonds'. A real masterpiece of the creative partnership between Elton and Bernie Taupin.

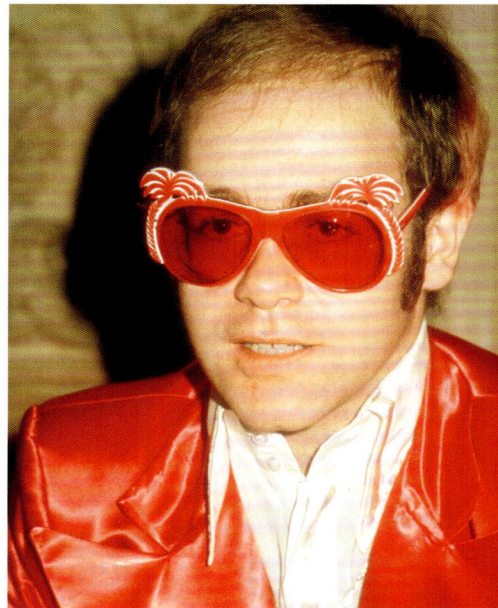

With Cher & Diana Ross

With Ringo Starr

BRYAN FERRY & ROXY MUSIC

LED ZEPPELIN

Their album this year 'Siren' was driven by the disco inspired 'Love Is The Drug' song that is a high tide mark of the Roxy catalogue.

After nearly a two-year break, Zeppelin arrived with this super-ambitious double album. Landmark songs like 'Kashmir', 'Trampled Underfoot', and 'Houses of the Holy' stand out as musical beasts from this album. Basically, this album shows the band at the very top of their game.

BAY CITY ROLLERS

The band's second album helped them be taken that much more serious-ly, with much improved performances from the band and big songs like 'Bye Bye Baby' and 'Keep On Dancing' causing widespread appeal.

STATUS QUO

When the band released 'Down Down' from their 'On the Level' album, it showed they really meant business. The band's first UK number one song and an all-time classic that never fails to lift spirits with its dynamic riff and sing-along lyrics.

SLADE

CLIFF RICHARD

NEIL DIAMOND

With Glen Campbell

NOLAN SISTERS

FLEETWOOD MAC & STEVIE NICKS

BARRY WHITE

FRANK SINATRA

LEO SAYER

STEVIE WONDER

HARRY NILSSON

MILES DAVIES

CAROLE KING

BOB DYLAN

PERRY COMO

BRUCE SPRINGSTEEN

BURT BACHARACH

BOB MARLEY

BING CROSBY

NEIL YOUNG

ROY ORBISON

DIANA ROSS

With Berry Gordy

BARBRA STREISAND

ARETHA FRANKLIN

NATALIE COLE

CHAKA KHAN

CHER

STYLISTICS

CARPENTERS

NEW YORK DOLLS

TINA & IKE TURNER

ABBA

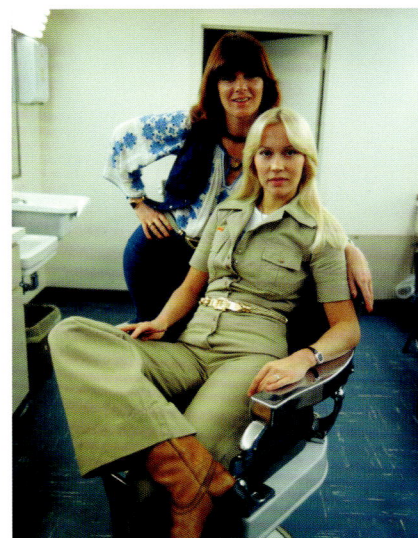

FASHION & STYLE

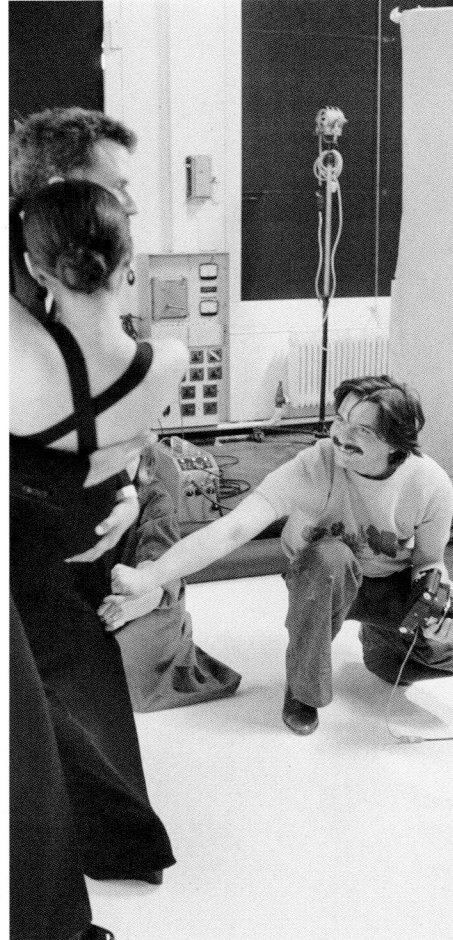

English fashion and portrait photographer David Bailey at Vogue's photo studios in Hanover Square.

Fashion models wearing some pieces from Mary Quant's new autumn/winter collection.

RADIO & TV

Stan Ogden of Coronation Street (actor Bernard Youens)

June Whitfield

Actor Michael Crawford

Comedian & actor Mike Reid

Lynda Bellingham with Greg smith & Robin Askwith

This year saw the debut of an amazing array of successful programmes. In January, 'The Sweeney' started; in February, 'Little House on the Prairie'; in March, 'Hong Kong Phooey'; in April, 'The Good Life' debuted, featuring Richard Briers and Felicity Kendal. 'Jim'll Fix It' began in May; 'Celebrity Squares' with Bob Monkhouse started in July; 'The Rockford Files' with James Garner in August; 'Runaround' with Mike Reid in September, along with the first episode of 'Fawlty Towers'. Finally, 'Bod', the animated TV series, started in December.

Norris McWhirter

Ronnie Barker

Ronnie Barker & Eric Morecambe

STAGE & SCREEN

JOAN COLLINS

HELEN MIRREN

DIAHANN CARROLL

LAUREN HUTTON

PAM GRIER

MICHAEL CAINE

SEAN CONNERY

DAVID NIVEN

TELLY SAVALAS

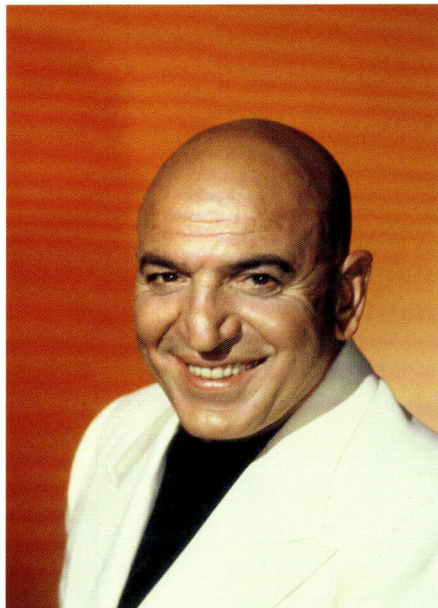

JACK NICHOLSON

With Angelica Houston

DUSTIN HOFFMAN

PAUL NEWMAN

IMAGE CREDITS

ALL IMAGES COURTESY OF GETTY IMAGES